LOVE + IT'S FRUSTRATIONS
COLLECTION OF POEMS

RA'CHARLES WHITE

LOVE & IT'S FRUSTRATIONS
COLLECTION OF POEMS
@Copyright 2021 by RA'CHARLES WHITE

All rights reserved.
No part of this book maybe reproduced or transmitted in any form or by any means without prior written permission from the author.
ISBN: 978-1-953638-14-4

**LIBRARY OF CONGRESS CONTROL NUMBER
2021907746**

Printed in the United States of America
This book or parts thereof may not be reproduced in any form, stored in a retrieval system, or transmitted in any form by any means-electronic, mechanical, photocopy, recording, or otherwise-without prior written permission of the publisher, except as provided by United States of America copyright law.

**PUBLISHER
TA MEDIA & PRODUCTIONS LLC
DALLAS, TX 75240
www.PUBLISHYOURBOOKTODAY.INFO
WWW.TAMEDIACO.COM**

AUTHOR BIO

I, Ra'Charles J. White (Ray) am a 43year old dual military veteran Navy & Army, who started passion for writing at tender age of 12. I come from a huge family where I begin to gather inspiration and love for my gift. Growing up on south side of Chicago I tried to steer towards sports, but the arts was definitely a hidden talent. This particular talent was noticed by my freshman English teacher. This notice soon awarded me to enlist at the time in "The Young Chicago Authors." I began the process of working on a journal of poems after sudden loss of my mother at age of 14. Through a variety of life changes I continued to write and bless loved ones with this gift over the years via personal or through sympathy during loss of loved ones. Many of these lessons I learned through all types of relationships; whether family, friends, or failed relationships; fueled this project and finally I have reached the goal or title of an author. I would like to thank first and foremost God with granting me such a gift, my entire family too many to name but all my siblings, nieces, nephews, cousins, aunts, and uncles, who helped push me. My closest friends since age of 4-21 who we still hang and keep it 100 with each other. To all my associates or fam at time throughout HS, college, Navy Days, Army, and countless coworkers met along the way. And lastly but definitely not least; I'd like to thank my wife to be Sirlina E. Stewart for giving me the drive to finish and make this work of art a reality. Her push allowed me to be more professional and marketable and without you baby I do not know if I'd even be here... so thank you $tack$!!!

I appreciate anyone who supports my dreams and welcome to my world. Peace and love and God Bless You!!!

v

TABLE OF CONTENTS

Family Love 1

From Momma: Family Togetherness 3

A Special Person In My Life! 5

Sweet Olé Brother Of Mine 7

Gone But Not Forgotten (Jesse "Charles") 10

For My Sister Tee (Tatiana) - A Brotherly Love 13

Greatest Dad Of All Time 15

Sweetness Of Auntie Bert 18

The Legacy Of Ray 21

Lena's Smile 24

For Randy (Grandma Susie) 26

Sweet Sis 28

My Name Sake 30

I Need A Reading 34

Not The Same Mother's Day 36

Mom's Love 39

Brother's & Sister's Keeper 41

True Friends 44

Open Mind 47

Black Love 51

Family Ties 54

Parental Rights 57
Praying Hands 60

Different & Disturbing Love 62
Bad Choices 64
Abuser 67
Cancel Everything Else 72
One Crazy Day 75
Beware The Curse Of Haters 79
Is It Worth Your Life? 82
Failure Is Not An Option 84
Pivot Point 87
Mentally Screwed 90
Shipmate To Warrior 92

Sex & Relationship Love 95
Love Lost And Lesson Learned 96
No Judgments 99
Act Right 102
As Shady As Can Be 104
Date Night 107
Dirty Secrets/ Fantasy (Xxx Warning) 111
Downtown And Beyond 115
Exes Are Exes For A Reason 118

For Hire!! 121

Good Side / Bad Side 125

How Do You Like Your Love Served? 128

How We Spend Our Time 131

I Submit To The Terms And Conditions 134

Love Or Insecurity 138

Intuition Or Intrigue; Searching Or Discovery ... 140

Indecent Proposal 143

Ingredients For Romantic Pastry 144

No Romance Without Finance 147

Rejection Is Not The End 151

Side Piece 155

Streaming Live 159

The Crush 168

Wandering Eyes 171

I Came; Did You 175

FAMILY LOVE

From Momma: Family Togetherness

Family togetherness is just a wishful dream

It is something we all eventually hope for

But in reality, sometimes things will never be as they seem

Some people stand on the outside kindly looking in

Though that open door that we left ajar

In order to bring our togetherness our way must make a drastic change

We must put aside our differences more or less

Please be more considerate of others without causing pain

Maybe family togetherness will be the final outcome

Let the new days ahead begin

We'll come together; we'll become friends

With so much love around us, with plenty more to spare

There will be Togetherness in our home

And so much love to share

Ida White
June 11, 1992

A Special Person in My Life!

Gave birth to me in 1977,
In 1992 she went to heaven.
The memories left behind so unique,
The love that she gave; so tender and sweet.
My mom is the one of who I write,
Her soul is flowing through the heavenly light.
Ida Mae was her name,
She had many friends, family, and lots of fame.
The children she had is a perfect six,
All together a big loving mix.
The great big family so beautiful and smart,
Her love, memories, and life so deeply drove into our hearts.

August 15, 1992

Sweet Olé Brother of Mine

His troubles and worries are finally over,
For the lord has called him home to join the others.
No more suffering or pain that had hurt us all,
For he has gone to the great heavenly walls.
Sorrow will come and time will pass,
Don't sit there and cry, just think of the happy days that you spent together that won't outlast.
You were the first of six,
Those kids were the best of picks.
His 3 sisters and 2 brothers who he led on,
Listened and enjoyed each one of his songs.
His father who loved him so much,
Is now going to send his son to his mother's lovely touch.
For his dad is the one who showed him manhood,
For all should applaud him he did Damn Good!
For we are not saying goodbye but good journey,
That God has chosen him heavenly and worthy.
So, we say good journey to these wonderful 33 years,
Love for our shouts and memories for our tears.
Sweet Olé Brother of Mine I say this last but, not least,
You led the path for Crystal, Gwen, Loucynda, Eric, and me.
For your memories are safe, like money in the bank,

We love you sweet brother; lovable, Olé gullible Hank!

July 1995

Gone but Not Forgotten (Jesse "Charles")

Gone but not Forgotten, the twenty-three years of my life that you embraced,

Knowing the memories are golden and cannot be replaced.

Though you made it hard for me at times in my childhood past,

Yelling at me and my friends playing, to get out the grass.

We thought of you to be an evil old man,

But at that time, we didn't understand.

The time it took to keep it looking great was something else,

We soon found out as teenagers, cause not too long after we had to do the work ourselves.

A lesson indeed was taught and learned as well,

As we began to grow in our minds, all the time you were really swell.

You embarked on us memories we now consider unforgettable,

Your family and friends will always consider you Mr. Reliable.

Some of my friends always asked me why you were so mean and tough,

I guess that makes a man in this world, that we sometimes consider rough.

The kind of uncle you were hard to explain,

The only word that comes to mind is Great because you always knew how to maintain.

Gone but not Forgotten is a title within itself,

So, let's not bow our heads in misery, he is not being put on the shelf.

He is just taking the next step towards finding that spiritual peace,

For God has called on him to join his family to be reborn and not to be deceased.

So, if you have a tear in your eye that's alright, if you are going to cry go ahead cry out loud,

For we are not here to mourn, we are here to celebrate his homecoming, so let everyone stand joyful and proud.

Gone but not Forgotten, my uncle is just singing a new song and dancing a new dance where the music does not pause,

So, let's give him what's well deserved, let's give him a great round of applause.

March 2001

For My Sister Tee (Tatiana) - A Brotherly Love

It wasn't long ago, when I met her warm embracing smile,
Even though her mood changes often, like that of Wild-Child.
Still in fact, she would tell you like it is,
That's what I loved most about her and made her my lil sis.
Not bound by blood, but friendship, was good for us,
I would fight any of her battles without hesitation or fuss.
Times would come and go, of us playing a game of spades,
But as we did that or anything else a deeper bond of love was made.
From watching videos or just going outside to chill,
We always enjoyed ourselves to keep it simply real.
From Samaria dancing, just like Tee, or saying something off TV,
We would laugh for days, and Tee was as proud as she could be.
She struggled a lil bit, but did a damn good job too,
She raised her daughter great and loved her through and through.
She doesn't leave behind sorrow, yet she leaves behind a legacy,

Family, friends, and loved ones that will fulfill her wishes and most desirable dreams.

We are all in sorrow and saying it wasn't her time,

For she was young, beautiful, and of excellent mind.

No more pain, tears, struggles, or anything else she might have had that hurt hurts her well-being,

God has called her home and her prayers have been answered and she is now receiving the ultimate healing.

The Godmother of my unborn child I say to you; "thanks for being a sweet dear friend",

I'll love you forever till I prepare to see you again.

A Brotherly Love brings me hear this day, to celebrate a life so young and true,

If I never told you before, I'll say it now, I always have and will forever Love you.

July 22, 2002

Greatest Dad of All Time

Once upon a time lived a wise great man,

Who met a blooming and lovely woman?

They moved once and had two kids,

Following his sister around town he was bound for a big bid.

Moved again and soon came another two,

Three girls and one boy; what is a couple to do.

Now his older sister moves yet again,

This time to the Eastside, where the lake is blocks from within.

This time the puzzle adds another two,

Two highly active boys which makes a sitcom tale seem really true.

No more moving he proclaims because anymore kids could be rough,

For a blue-collar kind of guy any more would be extremely tough.

Now he wasn't perfect, but he gave his all,

Six aspiring children would make any dad walk tall.

He gave his all to make sure we had the best of everything,

Even if it was not top of the line, it always seemed as if lived as kings and queens.

We were his princesses and princes in a court built for success,

Such a good team we left no room for stress.

We first lost our queen which hit us hard in the heart,

But as any good king, he remained firm and kept us from straying apart.

Then came the oldest prince to which he, the king, thought he lost control,

But as the great father he was, he had his court behind him; strong and bold.

Now my dad was known for his kindness and warm-hearted wit,

But mostly respected for his desire not to quit.

His legacy lives on through us all,

Five remaining children, three granddaughters and eight grandsons.

To some he was known as Junior or Uncle Junior Boy,

Being a gentle giant was one of his greatest joys.

We are not saying goodbye but rather welcome again,

For God has brought you to him to rejoice without the aches and pains.

January 2nd, 2005

Sweetness of Auntie Bert

For 30+ years the 7600 block of Saginaw was her home,
She was a pillar to the community her persona stood alone.
Her grace and elegance and beauty such a far,
If Hollywood walk of fame was in Chicago, she definitely would have a star.
From working at Leaf factory, oh those candy treats,
Making all the kids crave that sugar high sweet.
Tons of goodness wrapped in such a small frame,
Playing bid whist with family on New Year's I had my deck, thought I was a part of the game.
For myself, siblings, cousins, kids, nieces, and nephews alike,
That cookie jar changed shape but not the sweet delights.
If we were playing outside and she had a task you could do,
Our friends would say "we'll help we want some cookies too!"
When she had a chore from taking the trash cans out or dusting furniture or cleaning around the house,
We all broke our necks to get that pocket lint out.
Whether it was candy, cookies, freeze pops, or pocket change for the week,
With Aunt Bert there for you always expect a treat.

The snapping of fingers at healing; to her looking gorgeous in many designs and styles,

The older she got I'd swear she was shopping like a child.

"Get of my grass!" When we were just being kids playing in the yard,

Seem like it was yesterday the memories of the perfect sweetheart.

I speak for myself and my family, but our friends can contest,

Because she was a warm heart and extremely one of the best.

If you weren't a blood relative but was around a lot,

She was your aunt too and man did she play the part.

So, for the goodness and sweetness of such a beautiful soul,

Let's smile, enjoy a sweet or two, and make her memories as fond as gold!

September 2010

The Legacy of Ray

From Mississippi roots, to mean streets of Chicago, to the California coasts,

James "Ray" Lucas made it the most.

From Jimmie Lee's stable to Uncle Sam's military barn,

Ray served us all, always with open arms.

My uncle is a strong reason for what and who I am today,

Momma I thank you, for honoring your brothers: Jerry, Charles, and Ray.

My name is sacred and royalty in all the same light,

This legacy last on through every passing day and night.

For the gifts he brought every visit his heart warm and never lost its heat,

A giving man that was hard for many to compete.

For all my family I know we sorrow and hurt through these times,

But our family is rejoicing, for a reunion of a different kind.

Let's not say goodbye, instead it's a welcome home,

As we cross these tough roads; we definitely are not alone.

As I struggle with trying to reach the higher echelon of that of my Uncle Ray,

For I have the same name sake that my nieces and nephews would praise me the same someday.

So, I thank you for everything that you have done,
I'll keep the greatness of Uncle Ray going and be sure to pass it on!

April 2011

Lena's Smile

My heart is heavy and in mourn,

As the 3 sisters reunite a day reborn.

My Aunt has gone home to her mom her sisters and all love ones together,

For its the 1st of the month and it's their weather.

Aunt Lena tell my Momma and my Daddy I said hello,

Y'all bout to have a ball once again like playing with Jell-O.

So, to my family let us rejoice and sing,

As we all know she was a fighter and gonna miss the joy she would bring.

Wish it was more times I saw her, but all was worth every minute,

As her love and admiration, she had this is a family I'm glad I'm in it.

September 1, 2013

For Randy (Grandma Susie)

Family and friends; you truly value their Worth.

Cause when you think you're lost they got your back and your interests first.

As I send out a prayer and hug in holy spirit state,

Watch over the Graves family tonight; Lord for your will is at haste.

As Susie draws closer to your arms' I ask you guide them through these times,

Your will has been done though not of blood she will always be a special mom/grandma of mine.

So, look after Bridgette, Jackie, Nina, Holly, and Randy and rest of her great creed,

From the look of my eyes and others she done a great deed.

To my extended family you have my heart and warmth in this time of need,

Though not of physical sense I hope you take this blessing to heed.

I love you all and if there is anything you need at all,

James is calling her for next hand of spades or a hand of bid ...trying to win them all.

October 2013

Sweet Sis

Where art thou my prayers go; seem gone to a drift,

As my family goes on to a place of soulful bliss.

There's a party going on and it seems like I'm not invited,

For so many of my loved ones have transitioned and soon to be reunited.

As "Sis" goes on to join her mom and countless others who I cherish,

It's a celebration of sorts as we look on often as a perish.

To my cousins and Uncle, God knows what's in store,

For we often receive his message and dare ignore.

My heart is heavy for she was a second mom if truly didn't see,

Mrs. Margaret Robinson, I love you dearly and I'm going to miss your greens.

See you later auntie as I continue my journey of days to come and I can still hear you singing and lighting up a room,

So, we all have smiles to proclaim for you are truly a flower that bloomed!!!

January 2014

My Name Sake

For long as I could think back on days and years went by,

The name Charles Edward Robinson meant more than just some guy.

He constantly said thank you to my mom and dad for bringing him up to Chicago from Mississippi,

Those road trips to Greenwood as a kid seemed like an eternity.

I can recall the times he'd see a car with those plates and stop them on drop of a dime,

Asking "how is it back home"; not knowing who they were and kind of be out of mind.

But that's who he was for most it's just Rev without a pause,

But my first memories began as just simple Uncle Charles.

From the peanuts to toys to monetary gifts galore,

Whenever he came by, he made sure the nieces and nephews had more than we bargained for.

From the many Cadillacs to nicest of cars,

I wasn't sure for a while if my uncle was a movie star.

I saw for the first time on Douglas when I recall an angel in the midst,

He introduced her as Margaret most call her "Sis".

To the wedding at the lil Holy Starlight, remember the white building always had on the heat,

When Rev Blumenberg ask anyone think these two should not be married why of all people; my dad had to sneeze.

So as time came and he answered his calling became one the best speakers of God,

Weekend trips to church on the L was long and as kid quite odd.

But when I saw who my uncle became to be,

I begged my mom over and over can I join mommy, please mommy please.

She agreed and I came every week and would stay weeks at time during the summer,

When my mom fell ill Rev kept me close and made sure I wouldn't plunder.

This is when I realized my uncle had true meaning but at times, I did get silly,

From Me and Millie playing in basement and Charlie telling on us; " Millie Ray don't play with my ministry."

As I got older and started to follow my own path, I regret a lot of times I missed,

For he was my other dad and I often regret this.

But out of it all there was one constant that never gave way,

He'd always say regardless boy you know I love you, Ray.

So, there's me amongst his daughter and grandson carry his name,

Rev. Charles Edward Robinson is definitely in my hall of fame.

As his family grew from more than just blood you can see how much he meant,

So, these 67 years amongst us wouldn't you agree was time well spent.

I'm going to close with this so we can rejoice that his pain is over, but his memories live on,

" Get right church and let's go home!"

October 2015

I Need a Reading

From as early as I can remember I knew your gift was a treasure,

Your connection was set in stone, a messenger of God truly unmeasured.

Even though blood tied us into a bond,

Your wisdom and compassion were far from beyond.

My brother's God Mother; but to all of us a cousin; daughter of sweet Aunt Bert,

A minister of meta-physical teachings you surely sought out our inner worth.

Growing up some of my friends you didn't care for at all,

Yell and scream at us if a ball hit your car; you'd in essence punch a hole in a wall.

As time went along, you'd love and cherish my friends and soon they would be family too,

Your knowledge of so many of our family, I'd shake my head on inside and you speak names and, on the inside, "I'd be like who?'

With time comes wisdom we grew closer, and the love surely would cherish,

When I saw my darkest days, I'd stop by or call so you could hit my reset button and those thoughts soon to parish.

You would always say Pon-Pon; my mom; or dad always came to light,

Others at times came to share but you truly knew the real insight.

This not just my words but our family as a whole,

You confided with us all to seek our guiding light unlocking our inner soul.

Darline was your given name, but "Sugg" was who you were,

Sweet angel of a woman you delivered on so many occasions it was indeed good worth.

From the second cousins I can remember you taught lessons and gave healings and spoiled to heart,

From Zee-Bee to Andre'a to Lil John to Rayshon to Elijah a story for all of them ages far apart.

Memories will last forever for I will continue my breathing and flood myself so,

As we say goodbye to the physical; God and the others welcome you to their show.

At peace you are, no more pain or struggles; you're healed to capacity,

Save a spot for us all until we see each other again at the "Golden City!"

June 2016

Not the Same Mother's Day

So, for me at 4 my sister left for school I cried like she was mom.

At that same age, my babysitter left me in store and mailman Mr. Williams took me home and my mom was there on break and cried for my safety.

At 7 I cursed at my sister Gwen over some headphones when my Aunt Verna was on her way.

The beating I took with that plastic bat sticks to me this day.

Some many times as she stood her post as crossing guard me and Eric walked from Dixon and she embarrassed us so,

From her licking her finger wiping the rust of our faces to that infamous pinch holding back the cries as our friends looked on like whoa.

Then my 8th grade graduation came; and she willed her way to be there,

From my classmates to teachers the congrats I received, because they do not know,

How ill she was; what a miraculous show.

Then one year later the one I still feel today,

God had her come home for better she was cured this day.

So, for those who have their moms still at arms' reach,
Cherish her dearly for you don't won't to make this speech.

Mom's Love

Here's to all those responsible women who don't take the title for granted,

Conceived under some form of feelings outcome is definitely enchanted.

9 months of morning sickness body aches and crazy appetites of things not normally on her pallet,

Rubbing the tummy so is affection and true love that is dare unraveled.

I've miss mine since 1992 and these yrs. later it still hurts the same,

Wishing I could call out to her and in trouble even here her say my full government name.

The reason I'm caring, loving, and good provider is all due to one Ida Mae (Lucas) White,

As I see some people argue in discontent with their moms it's truly a hurtful sight.

Cherish your mothers for tomorrow is not promised to be all,

I wish I could pick up that phone for last call.

So, you Mother's beginning seasoned and elder alike this weekend I salute and my hats off to you,

Happy Mother's Day ladies this is your weekend for being Gods calling and so true!!!! 🌹🌹🌹🌹🌹

Brother's & Sister's Keeper

There's a lot to more to the label of being related,
Bound by blood or inseparable time through thick and thin you made it.
Whether it's from two people being in a marriage or just having those three minutes of intimacy,
A child is conceived an ultimate blessing they shall be.
The boy or girl is raised protected in their parent's arms,
Growing up without a care in the world they fear no harm.
Some of us has friends who treat us better than our own siblings do,
For this the term brother's or sister's keeper; is much more sacred and true.
To give your all to the relationship that's not like any other,
Sworn by the secrets, the troubles, but don't tell your dad or mother.
Fighting is there whether verbal or physical but draws you closer in,
Bound by blood or not truly your truest best friend.
Things you've seen and done are stories to tell or withhold,
At times when you recollect the laughter or tears never get old.
Am I my brother's or sister's keeper; yes, I am indeed,

For they are there when it matters most in my dearest time of need.

So, cherish thy brother or sister or both for some parents won't outlast,

Remember to full up that tank of love just like you fill your car with gas.

True Friends

You can be the man/woman who has that one true ride or die,

Been with through thick and thin don't sugar coat your faults; won't tell a lie.

There the one person you can't on to be there in your darkest hours,

Hold you up with support like the roots of a tree or flower.

Whether it's been a few years in or even a lifetime of running amuck,

Always got your back there when you need them to help you get unstuck.

The one person who gives you the sarcasm that you sometimes just can't stand,

But you have to laugh it off cause you're in agreement with their comments and just be like DAMN!!

Ride together, cry together, laugh together, there to help each other out in best and worst of times,

You have each other's back regardless never the type to drop a dime.

Loyalty truly like no other brother's/ sister's keeper; you definitely are,

Real to the ends of time; your Ying to their Yang by far.
So, honor your buddy, equal, ace boom coon, bro, or sis,
You have been there for another in's and out bond forged over memories can't even start to list.

Open Mind

First of all, let me tell you how I truly feel.

This is just a free style not really up to writing all the words down just want you to get the appeal.

A long time ago maybe about 26 years, I lost someone close to me who is truly, truly dear,

Not sure of my grandfather's maternal name but granddaddy Rogers is all I knew and my grandmother Ma Dea.

Then there's my brother at the age of 17 as I graduated high school,

By then I was already at a complete numbskull already acting a fool.

Had my son at the age of 25 I thought that would change things,

But before I knew it the woman that conceived my son, she was the wrong choice and I already gave her an engagement ring,

Two years later I lost my dad the last true tree that I had to lean on,

From here on out I knew that of course it would change to my lifelong theme song.

Been mentally disturbed since the beginning of these times,

Some who know me; especially over the last couple years wonder why my third always seem to come up blind.

I've been battling this mess for the last 20 years plus,

From running the streets, trying drugs, to do anything, they can make a person fuss.

If you want to know my life story this is a brief bio that you dare cannot ignore,

For what I have left to say please take heed to what I have in store.

Am I a child of God? Yes, I am indeed,

But everybody battles their demons somehow, we soon take heed.

For me it was in my early years when I was ignorant and didn't want to hear anyone's advice,

They knew the answers to what was true, and I should really run my life.

But as they say I was young dumb and full of cum; trying to fit in,

Living in my life and torture and misery; truly the ultimate sin.

From street narcotics and alcohol binges that left me up all night,

To me wondering what I can do next to pick the biggest fight.

To high numbers of encounters that would truly blow your mind,

Too many close calls of being burnt that I had to consider the doctors find.

Not perfect at all as I describe my life in a nutshell,

You make the most of your opportunities and follow your first mind decisions you might turn out swell.

If you second guess and contemplate what you need to do along your path,

You'll regret along your days like me and wish you'd truly know God's wrath.

So, pray, repent, fellowship as you try and try again,

The ultimate victory is when God see's you again.

Black Love

To Christina aka Chrissy aka Peanut and Christopher, I wish you both the best.

As you take a journey of companionship to the ends of final rest.

Life partners, back bone, better half, spouse, or whatever name you like to claim,

Just remember your vows and commitment and adapt to any sudden change.

To niece I watched you grow from that spoiled lil brat crying about anything to woman who's in control of her well-being.

I remember like yesterday running you and your friends around to school, parties, and so much more.

I'm proud of you peanut these tears I can't ignore.

To Chris take care of well I know you're a good dude and would do what's needed,

Ever need anything this end her dad, uncles, and cousins phone call away shall you need it.

This partnership brings forth something so exquisite and yet some of us hate to let go,

For your truly the woman and man we're proud of can't wait til your 50th anniversary if I'm around to see how much your love grow.

To my niece and now nephew I raise this glass to you for your love is awesome and admirable something so true!!!

Love you both,
Uncle Ray
October 14th, 2019

Family Ties

What keeps a family together is an age-old question we still seek answers to,

Who does it start with the grands, parents, aunts' uncles, or the new baby you call boo-boo?

Needless to say; it doesn't matter at times who keeps you all close or tied by blood,

It's what you do for each other in times of need, on occasion, or every day with a hug.

We grow older some get distant or stay close good bad or ugly fights alike,

From weddings, to funerals, to new additions to family things for these moments makes things right.

We often say we gotta do more spend more time together visit more often so forth and so on,

How many say they stick to that plan, that's a dragged-out long song.

It's true we say it some act more than they say without hesitation,

A lot of us have our individual families or current situation.

But family is always there when you need them in the darkest or happiest of times despite any distance,

I'm sure someone can I feel you and give their own disposition.

I like it when sis/bro did that or cuz remember back when,

Family is always there to embarrass you in front of your friends.

We cry, we joke, we fight, we do it all, as that what life brings,

Enjoy your family close and distant to your greatest means.

I can personally say we're not all close in mines; for our patriarchs and matriarchs alike, majority of them are partying up above,

But we continue their legacies; the best way imaginable; as you raised us all; with true unconditional love.

Parental Rights

For everyone out there who think having a 9-5 is all there is,

For us of those who have kids it's an 24/7 365 biz.

Married couples or single parents indeed we have big shoes to wear,

For caring for our offspring is tedious, consuming, and stressful and a lot to bare.

We take on this task sometimes it's chosen others by that one mistake,

But cherish and love our children no matter the stakes.

Praise when their good and punish when they misbehave,

For I miss the times of whooping's like that of a slave.

We change with the times and say not gonna raise our kids as parents did us,

But looking back we turned out alright despite all the fuss.

Why is it things are worse off now; than they were back then,

It's because society has taking the parents right to discipline accordingly with that swift backhand.

I'm not saying every situation or child deserves a that nature of correction,

But look at the generations before us and our current situation.

Kids have no respect and just sometimes do as they please with no remorse,

But when it hits the news or public's eye "oh he/she was good kid" knowing damn well that wasn't their course.

So real parents stand up for those of us who made our kids scared of us instead of emotional mess,

For those who came before us knew what was best.

Crime rates are high not for any other reason but what I state,

It always starts at home before they travel out that front or back gate.

Spareth' the rod; spoil the child holds true meaning back to biblical times,

For this is way of man centuries gone by with respect and humility in mind.

So, to have real parental rights is to be stern and effective where your child knows no means of disrespect,

For those of us who have done a great job parenting verbal; maybe physical know the truth of this context.

If your child has grown to the adult who you can brag about and be proud of head held high on,

This poem isn't for you because you listen to all the right songs.

Praying Hands

My prayer for new year is to daily be a better father, a better brother, better uncle, a better nephew, a better cousin, a better friend than I have been in past. I've been told recently by haters and those that have used me not all for bad that I whine and complain too often of my downfalls and not acknowledge my blessings. So, I say to you my lord, family, and friends help me along the way to this journey yet untold as I embark on this new year of life let me be better. I want to grow mentally, physically, spiritually, and financially so that I can be who I am destined to be. And no longer stress about the minor issues in life that detour me away from my lifelong goals. Dreams are dreams but actions are set in stone so the actions of this year of life let them be the bricks of the foundation I desire and lead me to the long sought after treasures I seek in life.

DIFFERENT & DISTURBING LOVE

Bad Choices

A little bit of truth is needed to explore this mindset,

From the minds of most people who sometimes make decisions they may regret.

Could it be a purchase or spending you know you didn't have any reason making?

But when you saw the item or chance thought it was ripe for the taking.

Instead of going with your clear state of mind you went with that gut feeling,

After the fact you put yourself in a whole and looking back what was real reason.

Sometimes we gamble away a means without anything to show,

Should've kept your ass away and strictly said no.

Or there's that person who looks good on the outside but inside an overall mess,

Despite all the warning and caution signs you feel that being alone is not being blessed.

They drain you financially, emotionally, and even physically at times with the scars to match,

But you love them, or they love you; you say such a wrong batch.

Tolerance for their bullshit you endure time and time again,

The hurt they cause drives a wedge between you and your family and friends.

Why the idiocy or personalities can't be a label on their forehead to display,

Well, this isn't no perfect world we live in, and we learn much to our dismay.

Craziness of all the bad choices come to light as some or often done in the dark,

It's ok to just sit and silence gather your thought and keep your ass in park.

We endure the bad, so we know what it's like to have things good come across our path,

And when it's said and done, we look back at these choices cry a bit but have a good laugh.

Abuser

Conflicting details as the detectives makes their cases,

Testimony of intrigue tears of pain from their victim's faces.

She was only 16 smart and beautiful, blossoming into a gorgeous young lady,

Thought of her innocence taken away drives a sane person crazy.

She looked up to her assailant as a remarkable figure,

But deep down he had demons that over- turned his nature into a sex crazed trigger.

She always came over to look after her elderly Nanna,

But this was her uncle by blood so she wouldn't believe the idea of him go bananas.

The older she got, the more her body took shape,

From a size 2 to double DDs, hips that could make an earthquake.

Besides this she was family and should have been protected,

He looked at it as an oversight and soon she became neglected.

From unwanted looks to touches to kisses and then the unthinkable thing,

How out of all imaginable possibilities, you rob her of her virginity?

Not even a boyfriend which she didn't even let get past second base,

The thought of him going that far she thought such a disgrace.

Now the second victim is definitely; not easy to handle at all,

He's a dual athlete looking to be about 6'6" tall.

Started with him out at Boy Scouts retreat,

Camping, hiking, swimming, fishing, cooking their own meat.

He was about 12 years old when this all began,

Not from a counselor but older brother of one of his closest friends.

He was an experienced scout who volunteered to help mentor junior minds,

But somehow along the way he began to mentor something of a different kind.

Took extra notice of the athletic prowess of this young scout,

Physically doing more teaching doing the swimming exercises at first no doubts.

Thinking it was normal cause had trouble as if he would drown,

But soon after he got it when they play dunked each other he was always close around.

Then there was double tents and he always knew it be him and his best bro,

But somehow the change suggested by the brother to switch it up began this unthinkable flow.

He was fast asleep and camp site was calm with crickets and nature calling,

Awakened by force of a bigger body resistance was futile with all the sprawling.

I don't like boys, don't touch me like that, get your mouth off of me he proclaimed,

He says shh before you wake the rest of the camp this is only a game.

Went on for an hour or so; unable to sleep the rest of the night away,

When morning struck; he told the counselor he was ready to go home and that's all he had to say.

No mentions to the Nanna for the young lady didn't want to contribute to her illness,

But as she got home and told her parents mom called the police; dad grabbed shotgun said I'm kill that "son of a bitch!"

The boy returns home much to the head scouts dismay for long trip back,

Said he wasn't feeling good and just left it at that.

Immediately when he walked in door rushed in room full of tears,

His mom and dad said what's wrong my dear?

Parents were angry as ever and full of content,

Easily to say the camp site was shutdown ASAP without any hesitant.

These cases come dime a dozen and often unsolved because closeness of who attacker is,

Remember face your fears and keep mindful who's around your kids.

Cancel Everything Else

I don't get to express the way I feel cause of daily routine,

We converse mostly about what to do business wise lately and I struggle to tell you what I mean.

You're my sunrise and sunset for that I cherish dearly,

You put thoughts in my head that I erase but I act on them severely.

No actions taken other than a message here out of the blue,

For I recognize that I'm truly deeply in love with you.

You're my queen indeed and I treasure you so,

To ends of Earth, I'll take that journey just to let you know.

We fight so much lately for lack of us being apart,

So, close we are but due to circumstances we still are so far.

I can't imagine not truly bowing down to your grace and taking one knee,

Presenting you with a ring and asking you to marry me.

So, if there's a chance in hell, we can overcome this debacle I pray it is so,

For forever I'd be happy as you are my ultimate show.

The woman I intend to spend rest of days on this Earth admiring and taking to moon and back,

As I apologize for my failures and do nothing more than pick up your slack.

We both have issues that can be overcame as we work well as a team,

Our love is great on one accord the perfect dream.

So, I say special woman in my life for this final thought I put before you as we've fought so hard to be,

My words I express now we ride this wave out if you truly love me.

Issues definitely will arise, and we will knock down those walls as neither of us is perfect,

But let's just sit, think, and contemplate; is it really worth it.

I want you and only you and show out just to give you notice,

I apologize for my deceit and love you and only you for I hope you know this.

Sacrifice has been made time and time again,

I rather have you as my mate, partner, lover, and if not, I don't think it will work as a friend.

Friend yes only if we're laying next to each other 20-40yrs from now until God all mighty decides,

So, I'm game if you are to take this ride!!!

One Crazy Day

Woke up as usual and you're feeling pretty good,

Same old routine head to work nothing left to be understood.

On the way in a homeless guy walks up to car reeking in funk,

You quickly slide him some change so by time he says thank you he's pass your trunk.

Good deed done but couldn't take the smell,

Onward you proceed but then approaching next scene like "what the hell!"

You see it happen right before your eyes,

As this is a bit disturbing and ultimately a greater surprise.

An accident with people walking across the street and a girl fleeing out a moving van,

You're not even on the clock yet but your duty as a detective now you have to come up with a plan.

You call it in and describe the scenario to 9-11 dispatch,

Before you know what's really all the moving parts you just have to react.

Access the damage, victims, and whose truly at fault,

For the girl you seen running goes into a Starbucks hurdling the fence like Olympic pole vault.

You stop the van she was in and see the driver shaken up but bloodied by impact,

But failed to see the pedestrian that got struck due to this crazy react.

As patrols and EMTs arrive; other bystanders close by who acted on instinct saved time and lives,

Your stress is down a bit and can focus on the incident and now investigate the cause of your crazy morning drive.

You ask all victims what they saw those that were coherent and such,

Gather statements pass along to other officers and then remember the girl in Starbucks.

She's shaking and scared and keeps proclaiming don't let him find me,

You ask her; her name; the shock of her identity.

A congressman's daughter whose been missing for few years,

As you hear it yourself you can't help it but to break out in tears.

You radio dispatch and tell them to call detectives/ officers at hospital for victims coming in,

Hold the driver of the van for he's responsible for an abduction and this accident becomes bad but turns into a win.

Family reunited after an intersection accident,

You'd never thought you be center of news across the nation if such an event.

Awards reign in and talk shows and producers all want your story,

A crazy day it turned out to be, but you proclaim to "god be the glory!"

Beware the Curse of Haters

It may just be jealousy or something they don't understand,
That's those on the outside looking in can't quite comprehend.
Your happiness is contagious, and it draws other close,
You don't brag or act conceited you just have a spirit that's genuine to most.
Your desire is much to be desired and cherished frequently by all friends and family,
Some have broken their necks to reason out to you just to be close to thee.
You're just a fun person, energetic, and warm to the darkest of people,
Your story is quite unusual if those who knew the truth be something of a horror sequel.
But you cast those dark corners aside and extinguish any lingering demons that come your way,
You've been down that path before but with right support and prayers you're now winning and know every counteraction to their negative play.
But then there's the ones on the outside try to stir up gossip and trouble,
You bob and weave their attacks and steady hitting triple doubles.
Let them hate on you and try to tear you down like so,

For their bringing themselves down and can't steal your glow.

Instead of admiring and seek out advice of how you move the way you do,

They criticize and keep up nonsense because they have nothing better else to do.

This could coworkers, associates, past fail relationships, and even baby daddies/ mommas,

But you're too good for nonsense and keeping swerving all that drama.

You keep your content and maintain your foot on the gas for things to come that's greater,

Just remember these words I say, "Haters make you Greater!"

Is It Worth Your Life?

Here's an argument that can be seen as a debate,

Life struggles can have you questioning your own faith.

Whether it's finances, employment, or family/relationships gf/bf; husband/wife all the same.

The path you choose or don't choose eagerly God and Satan began the tug of war game.

So much to live for you have this, you have that, blessed more than others,

But yet when you think you're doing good the troubles begin to smother.

From having house, job, car, steady income, or world of riches,

Some less fortunate just pray they had a sink of dirty dishes.

Stressing cause this bill ain't paid, or behind cause had to get kids this or he/she lie or cheated,

Some just out here struggling for next meal, an overcrowded room perhaps instead under a bridge where at least it's heated.

I've traveled this dark path far too many times to count on one hand,

Just fortunate enough to outlast the devil's temptation and indulge in his demand.

Not sure when I go but I have leave something memorable and decent behind,

Instead of why he takes his life with so much accomplished leaving nothing but troubled and puzzled minds.

So, if that darkness rises its head more than you like seek guidance in those you trust and love,

I'd prefer not spending my life in depths of hell instead of the heavens above.

Stress kills they say I'm beyond my boiling point and can't take no more,

Is there anything else in this world for me to discover and explore?

Failure is Not an Option

This is a saying that a lot live by no matter the circumstances,

Whether you're in a profession, relationship, financially, family, or learning a new dance.

It comes off so cliché that it's hard to abide by at times,

For you do not know what your future holds you only react to what's seen that once was blind.

It can be trying to win a game to get to the playoffs to win that championship,

There is no I in team, but this day in age we idolize superstars and too often forget.

You want that new job so bad your resume is on fleek, and you have the credibility,

You land that spot work hard but now that promotion you've accepted turns out to be a liability.

You put your money away starting off small loose change a dollar here and there til you get to the hundreds and now you're over a stack,

But Wham!!! An unexpected turn of events, and you must start over and no point of looking back.

You keep close relationships with friends and family and raise your kids well,

Who'd of think it that after all the preparation and dedication you put forth; you're visiting your child in jail.

You lived a healthy lifestyle took your vitamins, played sports, and worked out regularly,

Now you're hit with these test results that you're thinking that's positive "oh no not me!"

You have all your dreams and aspirations taking you on a roller coaster of sorts twist and turns,

You've felt the good, the bad, the ugly, the cold, frozen, and the burn.

Now you're looking in the mirror asking yourself; what can I do next,

Just remember you say your prayers, you're repentful, a child of god, and you're truly blessed.

Pivot Point

It's the reaction that's made from good things to come or bad things that happened,

Whatever the case you have put forth solid effort so that you can embrace the reaction.

From costly decisions that can affect your whole lifestyle,

To one false sense of self you turned into that forgotten child.

As you contemplate what it is you desire, want, and need,

Your surroundings begin to crash and adverse reactions take heed.

So, what decision do you make that other responses don't solidify who you truly are,

As you make these necessary steps, you're being true to yourself and ultimately your own number one star.

Life deals us punches yes this is facts, but we must know how to adapt,

No need for sorrow or self-pity it's time to counterattack.

You're the biggest enemy you'll face from birth to adolescent to adulthood and all areas in between,

Beating yourself up will only bring you to a devastating end and crush all your valued means.

Words hurt and actions leave marks, but this is just a phase,

We're born all the same beyond whatever your belief is it's in the most high's grace.

So, call to your spirit ask for forgiveness of sins old and those to come, cry, pray, and be best you can be,

Our creator understands we're not perfect in his eyes he knows what to truly see.

So, relax, deep breaths, meditating or smoke you a joint,

Just remember you are the true navigator to your Pivot Point!

Mentally Screwed

What's is it about memories that draws our attention to be so jacked,

Is it bad relationships, deaths in family, financial issues that damn near gives us a heart attack?

From growing up as kids all of us say I wish I could turn back the hands of time,

To change that one instance to stop that mistake at the drop of a dime.

It was easier then, carefree, and not a bill in sight,

For those of us that wasn't teenage parents it was true delight.

Could live like no tomorrow and still just maintain and enjoy being a kid,

Then adulthood hit; oh, fuck responsibilities, bills, job, damn gotta get my own crib.

College was a blast if you attended the party the guys, girls, games, and frats,

For some it was staying at home, still continuing to be a brat.

Then there were those who did the ultimate and swore to defend the freedoms and put into that uniform,

Travel halfway across the world places extremely nice, cold, or warm.

Reality sets in when you hit a certain age 25,30,40,50 and so on,

Wondering if anything you did in life was ever truly wrong.

Always contemplating about the what if's and should did that different versus this,

Now it's just a matter of sucking it up it was a life decision and either hit or miss.

So, for to struggle is to achieve as to win is to lose,

Don't forget to ignore that button on the next opportunity for those who ain't following I'm talking about the "snooze!"

Shipmate to Warrior

14 yrs. it takes for most to become a teenager to adulthood,

For me, this journey took me to places I didn't quite know back in 1996; what it understood.

Looking back from my days as a swabee, from 3 stack bunks, Dixie cups and dungarees,

To molly rucks, FTXs, ACUs, to a good old M-16.

Places I've seen I can't say been on any other accord,

Eastern Europe, the Mediterranean, Caribbean, Canada, West Coast, on my dime definitely couldn't afford.

I'm grateful for the lifetime of lessons learned and taught in same breath,

I wish I could say I had just a little bit left.

But my time has run its course and I serve my country well,

Still wearing the same the same rank suits, me swell.

It bothers me a bit; but I never let it keep me down,

As I stayed true to the values and ethos and continued to the battleground.

So, I'm going to leave with this Wolfpack; you need me I'm a phone call away,

To the 1744th I thank you for this journey and there's only one thing left to say.

So, count of 3; 1..2..3..

WHO ARE WE? Warriors! WHO ARE WE? Warriors! WHO ARE WE? Warriors!

Love y'all! Thank y'all!

SEX
&
RELATIONSHIP
LOVE

Love Lost and Lesson Learned

Consider there was an instruction manual on to be true to yourself and succeed,

Some maybe all would open this manual and follow it to the T.

But this is life and there's no situation that can prepare you for the next,

You first, have to look inside yourself and define your own texts.

Up and downs sure it happens it's called experience when it's all said and done,

The longevity of a relationship decades down the road defines if battle is truly won.

From finances, to infidelity, to jobs, to personalities, it's all part of the game,

Can't study them all because it's too much on the heart and brain.

Every situation brings forth a new challenge unlike the last,

But you have to learn how to move forward and not live in the past.

Yes, there's similarities and things you might just compare,

But don't treat the new love like the ex because this is a setup for failure you bet not dare.

Try to find what's truly your passion and upsides to offer this person you choose to take this path with,

For when you discover the real you and portray it that's the love you can present and that's a real gift.

Times we find ourselves questioning; what I can do differently to make this work,

If it's not suitable it's time to change subjects and do different type of homework.

Yes, you can be involved, in any fathom of the way imaginable to your hearts content,

But if the feelings, emotions, and actions aren't being reciprocated it's time to reinvent.

Not yourself because yes you can make a few changes but stay who you are,

For that true love maybe staring you down just around the corner and not very far.

If need help to discover don't be afraid to ask those that know you best,

We're all human that make mistakes no one is perfect with an S on their chest.

We can be great, but everyone has their flaws,

If you haven't discovered the real you don't force a situation; regroup and keep your feelings on pause.

Time will reveal who you truly are; and your soulmate awaits,

For we're destined for a certain type of love that's our true fate.

NO JUDGMENTS

Did you ever realize how often life changes your perception?

From the moment we're conceived there's no wrong direction.

So, this might come as a shock but many struggles with this idea,

As things have definitely changed and new customs dawn upon us each new year.

So, if you're born into your family room covered in sports memorabilia and decked out in blue,

Chances are your mom and dad called you son all the years they thought were true.

Or you were that fairytale princess pigtails or curls with flower dress dancing to and fro,

Pink was definitely the color of choice this much we do know.

But somehow along the way things get confusing and sexuality begins to take its place,

No matter what creed, religion, no bias on these fronts or race.

It was hidden throughout the years isolated in my many of our cultures and cities,

Hidden throughout our penal system and sight of it wasn't pretty.

Most cases when growing up abused, assaulted, molested, something sickening in that kind of way,

Things have definitely changed, and now it's more of a trend to be openly gay.

To each its own but Love has no color, shape, creed, or sex,

Just make sure when doing so; do it with some respect.

ACT RIGHT

Men, first off, let me tell you what my daddy always told me,

There's no winning an argument with a woman, so let's just agree to secretly disagree.

Secondly let's just put this to bed or start a whole another argument,

Cause she's always right with her emotions even though she's messed up NO fucked up with her logic.

Because that's the nature of the beast they think with their hearts too many times,

We use our brains first, but they say we are walking blind.

They say we think too much with the head in our pants but that's the one that get them to do that oh so naughty dance.

I believe women just love to see their men mad at them just for no reason at all,

Over the smallest and dumbest shit even if I said that kid over was only this tall.

Even on big issues it always comes down to their final word,

We sit there nod our heads, uh huh, ok, shaking, looking so absurd.

Why do we do torture ourselves through and through since the beginning of time,

Eve did it to Adam and we still ain't learn our lesson to this age-old rhyme.

We put up with the shenanigan's day in day out all over again,

Why? So, we can feel like we belong, and we have the title of being this woman's man.

Hmmm I say, something has got to give and just doesn't suit or fit,

Like the OJ case if the glove doesn't fit you must, must acquit.

But here's the solution and hear me out before both sexes reading this get all uptight,

Women put us through hell, fussing fighting, just so the sex, love making, can be that good ole nasty ACT RIGHT!!!

As Shady as Can Be

Let me tell you fellas how fortunate we have it in this world,

For every race, creed, and color there's a beauty I'm about to breakdown; pull up a seat I as take you for a whirl.

I'm going to start at home as there's many different flavors and desires can't ignore,

The African American woman different shapes sizes, and colors beauty destined to explore.

Got that hint of vanilla, to caramel, to cinnamon, to chocolate, to that luscious mocha Swiss,

Damn these are options; too many to choose from, take your pick of this visual bliss.

To the Latina sensations or my Boricuas that have that spiciness of appeal,

To the coconut delicacy, passion fruit, or butter pecan; I love a good deal.

To my Asian persuasions, subtle but in high demand,

Squinting of the eye's beauty like that of the sands.

Hazelnut or New York vanilla take your pick,

Islanders of East something kind of exquisite.

To my island woman of the West decent flavors light or dark,

Moving their bodies in ways; making the seas move apart.

Then there's the European treats that often get scrutinized trying to look like something they're not,

From simple to tanned let's just say tasty as an apricot.

Blonde, toffee, ginger, or strawberry choose your delight,

Seeing these options such an incredible sight.

All the beauty is not described as too many flavors to go through,

The essence of the female, God's greatest gift to man in my opinion, what can we do.

The nature of thy mother, daughter, wife, fiancé, or girlfriend,

A competitive status of beauty for this war will never end.

You can decide what you like, want, need, or desire,

Choose wisely my brethren as it's a task indeed and that job soon to hire.

Beauty so desirable and top of any scales maxed out to the extreme,

With such a smorgasbord of flavors make sure you have your #1 pick for your team.

Date Night

Such a great couple in the making from time they met,
Envied by others; and shown lots of respect.
Smiling from ear to ear every time someone sees them out and about,
If they had issues couldn't tell even from others word of mouth.
He is stern and confident and chest poking out walk y'all and proud as can be,
She moves in a way hips being thrown around face glowing like a star of eternity.
Friends close to them still try to figure out their secret of happiness,
Coworkers of both wonder how stressful the job s they have and no emotions of craziness.
Only together for a short year going on close to two,
The enchantment they have with one another so blissful and true.
To break down the secret one of coworkers observe and start to discover,
As the boss approaches the male about overtime and crunching the numbers.
He tells his boss no I'm good I took care of that task before my last break,
The boss in amazement but the figures I just looked at had to be a mistake.

He told him I can't deviate from schedule or mess up my plans,

For I take the work home with me and do it til I fall asleep so I can make our clients fully understand.

The boss looks at him so why do you work so hard without doing it on OT,

Because me and my lady have a date night set up that goes on weekly.

She does the same with her employer and they're shocked and amazed at her results too,

But we both said we are trying to do something different this go around so we know our love is true.

So, we sacrifice our sleep and hours throughout the course of the week,

But when Friday hits and no work talk it's just her and me.

The boss looks at him and said I come in on weekends thinking I'm slacking on our production,

But you just gave me the greatest idea on how to decrease our stress deduction.

Yes, it can drain a bit by weeks end but definitely worth it if you have a partner on the same grind,

Weekly date night for us is excellent and double added bonus with more bump and grind.

Boss chuckles and said how so true but do you guys fault from the plan,

Only when we're done early on a day and not exhausted, we try to get it in.

Date night once a week that's the key he asked,

Nope we do it once during the week at home our out just make it part of our tasks.

It's there just takes work and proper mindset to achieve,

He shakes his head agreement walks away calling his wife "honey u gotta tell you something you wouldn't believe."

Dirty Secrets/ Fantasy (XXX warning)

Let's put the kids to bed, put your feet up like so, and grab some popcorn for this show,

As you're now about to read something that's gonna make your juices flow.

The nastiest nature of something so extreme I can't take all the credit,

This is just past and things to come; a lot I can't seem to forget it.

It started when I had my first encounter with woman of older age,

She turned me on to more than just touchy feely; she had me on a whole another page.

From showing me the in's and out's and surrounding areas of her clit,

How to caress, touch, suck, bite, and even nibble it.

Then there was the way on how to please her so,

Licking her in every inch from head to toe.

Even in her anal cavity I thought eew this I can't imagine,

But when it's scrubbed down the right way it's an experience can't even imagine.

She sucks on me like so and not talking my penis,

She had me feeling something kind of squeamish.

She opened the door for things to come in my lifetime,

From try to please every woman I encountered and to this day I haven't dropped the dime.

From experiments with extras like lubes, ice, food condiments galore,

I still have a lot left in the tank to learn and even explore.

From toys in bedroom to sexy erotic hotel getaways where their built just for this thing,

In these scenarios you have to participate fully so you both can acknowledge each other's scream.

To that ultimate fantasy of things unimaginable that can erotically take place,

Having a gorgeous woman on my crouch another on my face.

Some women say that's selfish that two woman and one man and want the same thing,

Maybe for the right woman I'd share but this ain't that time and I'm running my own team.

But jacuzzi encounters, outdoor activities, backseat of car, and voyeur types of display all those I have to say check,

But what other fantasy can I portray or even say what's next?

Something to ponder as I reach out for that ultimate climatically experience,

Are you wound up with naughty thoughts or disgust cause you're not the one who thought of this?

Not trying to throw a shot or be too vulgar and have you turn your cheek,

We all have a wild sexual side inside its human nature I just put mine into words for you to read you don't have to speak.

My fantasies are my own and sure similar to some of you the same,

Be safe when you act on them because it definitely has mine going insane.

I love the taste, smell, and feel of woman I'm with to every nipple, dimple, and lip of her clitoris region,

Just be the woman I need for moment at hand, and I'll make sure I pledge allegiance.

Downtown and Beyond

Let's get started with the perfect situation,

A great night out on the town now let's take that erotic direction.

He's 6ft tall, dark, and handsome; she's a mouthful of curves, smart and independent,

Their night out; serviced like a star couple on the red carpet.

Dinner drinks play then dancing,

Ultimate end would be a night full of romancing.

What step is there next to do neither has a clue,

For all the signs are there each wonder if too good to be true.

His place or hers they both debates,

Getting a 5-star room is best solution as this is worth its wait.

Stop by package store to grab a lil extra to ease the tension,

Jacuzzi and all included in their room paying each other full attention.

All indiscretions are completely out the window,

Not sure whose to start this wonderful evening of ecstasy they both move slow.

Kissing commencing as if they were together for years,

However, this is their 4th date and they both had plenty of fears.

Now their stripping each other down to their birthday suits and making a heavenly mess,

Heated feelings and the steam is heavy not from the jacuzzi but from their bodies moving chest to chest.

He takes a breath and slowly goes down under the water line bubbles moving and relaxing her so,

She's like what the hell as he tastes her every inch of clitoral as water moves to and fro.

She tugs his ears like in fear of him drowning but he's good at what he do,

She's really not trying to explode with squirting as the water and her juices might be too much for him, but he says, "just let it go!"

They exit the jacuzzi and soon take heed to the bed for more pleasure to enjoy,

She's had two already and thinking to herself damn he's good; bye-bye my favorite toys.

She lays him down and tell him sick by now it's my turn,

He submits with ease as she slowly starts to wind and churn.

She licks his tip and slowly works down his shaft and testicles too,

Working like a lollipop he's noticing her tongue ring is hitting it like a fly to glue.

They both now have climaxed and are drained to a sense and want to precede feeling each other,

But this story will continue as it's for an act to take place under the covers.

Exes are Exes for a Reason

Why do we go through heartache and torment to suffer the days, weeks, months, and years for some even so?

The fact we let a person come into our lives and drain us of time, energy, and maybe finances stealing away a piece our growth.

They say you live, and you learn through every life lesson and can practice what you preach,

I wish there was lesson in school that can tell you the ups and downs of love this I'm waiting for them to teach.

You can't bring the past into current relationships as this cause for much turmoil and dismay,

But you often make comparisons even though not always intentional it's just learning from past mistakes in such a way.

But then there are those who present these experiences on consistent basis,

Whether it's saying how it was or they did this it's still wrong like a murderer on trial case.

Sometimes those have the ex-hanging around calls and pop ups still knowing your every move,

How are you supposed to grow with the one you with if the one you had still impressing you with their groove.

Leave the past in the past it's there for a reason and just keep thoughts and try something different ahead,

It's things of this nature that make a good person go bad that leaves much unsaid.

Can't keep them as friends or having them show up to your new location because this hurts what currently have,

Learn from your past mistakes and lessons and try to enjoy your life and have a laugh.

Exes get that gleaming array of hope as they still have a chance with you keep them at bay,

Oh, I'll talk to you later or see you some other time I'm chilling with my bae.

So those that like drama you'll continue on keeping up the same tradition,

But for those who learn that love and matters of heart are precious do a different rendition.

For Hire!!

Services rendered or balance paid in full is what we often see on a purchase,

In matters of the heart we have to take an in depth to look to solve this great purpose.

For women you're often picky to jump and not sure if his book is worth reading,

To find your Prince Charming you can't be shallow, or you'll miss the true feeling.

Not the best of physiques but he's working on being better,

Takes it old with romance gives you corny love letters.

Credit ain't great but he continues to show improvement has everything that's his own,

Takes care of the two kids he has from previous relationship but you've yet to let your mind be blown.

You grade him B+ at best sexually most because of his physical appearance,

But yet in still he delivers at drop of a hat all your tedious wishes.

You want to explore options as you're unsure if he can truly be your type,

To spend more than just the year you have together you contemplate and gripe.

For men it's different we're shallow a bit to say the least,

We want arm candy on our side built like Amazon a goddess of a beast.

We don't find out about the imperfections and all the baggage they have til date 2,3, or 4,

Somethings later are easy to deal with others can't ignore.

The ideal woman we seek own money, car, house, educated and all,

Easy on the eyes definitely imagination of all our nasty thoughts begin to crawl.

Then there's those that make it bad for others and create that unprecedented dog,

Have their hands out consistently want you to help with it all.

If you could help them breathe, probably ask for that too and act like their queens to be worshipped as so,

To deal with these type women need your cape and non-slip boots for your "Capt. Save A Hoe!"

So, to find the proper candidate for the position that you desire to be filled,

It's up to you to decide to do you want drama and turmoil or certain unique set of skills?

For women you want tall dark and handsome chiseled like a rock,

Only thing may be good for is showing you how to properly make your bed rock.

Or there's the ok looking guy who has head above the rest successful and good hearted,

He's the one you definitely can call when need car jump started.

For men it's quite the same but in different aspects as we lust often too many times,

To contort the body for you is nothing if she can't do the same with your mind.

Rather you like being the dominant in every step of the way that's cool,

Or you like an equal who takes no bs from simple minded fools.

Make sure you fill your opening with what matches your personality and every way of your life,

Maybe someday you can have that significant other as a husband or wife.

Good Side / Bad Side

Let me ask you a question would you like if people had their issues displayed on their forehead,

For you can determine instantly if it's worth it to spend time and effort to accept their faults without being misled.

This would make it easy for relationships and marriages that come to an all too familiar end,

As you could determine off back if you can be more than friends.

But that's not the case and you have to go into these areas quite carefully,

To understand what you can and can't deal with is something you have to trust in yourself truthfully.

From drama with baby momma's and daddies to past relationships still taking heed,

How do you determine if this can really succeed?

But then there's all the good thing this person possess,

From a career, to home, good with their kids, and bills paid, two cars looking fully blessed.

Such a great personality, good conversationalist, things are so at a bliss,

Even the romance is on point not close to a miss.

So can good outweigh the bad even if it's some things that's very dramatic,

These are questions you ask yourself as matters of your heart being torn apart can be tragic.

Trust in your spiritual beliefs and looks for the signs that point you in such a way,

Good side or bad side it's not written on the forehead at all but it's something we all experience and have to except without display.

How Do You Like Your Love Served?

Can it be a recipe that drives your mind wild,

Or the essence of feeling happiness like getting a new toy if you were a child.

This is questions that come to mind making you feel in ultimate bliss,

From the hugs, the touches, and gestures to that oh so meaningful kiss.

We all have distinctions of what make us feel in such a way bout those we want to love,

From head to toe we worship them in such a way that gives us that glow and fits like a glove.

For women it could be the strength a man provides and the dominant nature he brings to table,

Assertive in his every being, physicality is a must to put you in check at times to know you're stable.

He can be 6' tall cut like a mold out an artist's playbook or somewhat plump or big just you find you love how he looks.

Makes you weak to your knees with his deep commanding voice,

Ain't shallow or missing a beat in bedroom you know you have your number one choice.

For men we require a beauty always sometimes it's opposite from outside looking in,

We like to have some candy present, Coca Cola shapes figure thick, plump, or thin.

Hair doesn't matter cause beauty is in eye of beholder and doesn't really make or break us,

She can be cut short, medium, or long for it's what draws her to us.

Curvy no matter the shape or size definitely desire something to hold onto,

Then we dig inside her insides to see if it's the personality that matches hoping not too good to be true.

From dating, to ecstasy, to emotional connection, conversations of any topic we both can agree upon or disagree,

We find ways to make love work despite the smallest discrepancies.

For you find love that works for you and your content and happy to any imperfections your mate has,

You both fill up the others portion of life in once what was a half-filled glass.

So, you choose your life partner wisely and you both shall have memorable moments to share,

Just make sure you respect, honor, and trust your lover to the ends for you'll have that type of love can't compare.

A dish of this a dish of that and you have a well-made pallet put in your face,

You have the keys to your love make sure you're paying a mortgage with your heart date not rent this place.

How We Spend Our Time

We can take strolls down the beach,

Sit in the sand and just chill without a word to speak.

Sit around the house and just watch everything shows or movies laid up under each other,

Rubbing each other down snuggling under a cover.

Cook a meal together playing with the food as we prepare,

It may get a little kinky and even burn a meal or two cause the moment we didn't spare.

Ride our bikes down a path for miles at a time,

Watching the sunset or moon rise as we unwind.

Picnics in the park can be such a delight,

Or sitting on a terrace observing the twinkling stars light up the night.

Believing inside what our mission is really about,

Being true to one another without having any doubts.

We check each other for mistakes and compliment for awards,

Our togetherness is hot like that of liquid swords.

We can take a ride on a roller coaster and be thrilled to our hearts content,

We shared our time wisely and it was time well spent.

The best moment of all that will be the best of the greats,

We could get married where we met and roll down the aisle in our matrimonial skates.

I Submit to The Terms and Conditions

Let me set the stage so you can soak it all in,

This is not for the weak of heart or pants I should say for moisture don't keep it in.

Submission I endure as you have your way,

Speak only at your command is all you want me to say.

I'm bound and gagged; handcuffs but no mask blind fold will do,

As you begin your erotic torture, I'm in for a wild night this much is true.

Ice, fruit, whipped cream, edible solvents, and leather straps for disobedience if I act disobedient,

In my mind this is the perfect outcome for my pleasure with you is far from intermediate.

Anything goes except for the fact of you being treated in the same fashion,

I'm clueless at your intent for what's next about to happen.

You start with the ice as a tickling sensation takes heed,

Down to the adult edible solvents the intensity is much more than I need.

You touch and fondle me in ways that's hard for me not to squirm,

But the fact you say don't move the strap follows up for now I feel the pleasurable burn.

You tease with fruits and whipped cream bite I shall not do,

As you wanted me to only nibble a bad child, I'm being so you now must subdue.

You tell me to taste this and don't mistaken the flavor,

Correctly I answer your nipple, but your clitoris is doused with fragrance I definitely want to savor.

But it was hard to make the determination of so many collectible sweets,

As you've given much more than I bargained for truly all sensational treats.

As you begin to place your warmth on top of me and slowly glide in all types of motions,

The warning of me not climaxing too soon I take notice to this devotion.

As you take your time at first, it's making out to be your perfect scene,

But as you speed up a bit, I fear your warning might be faulty as my moans turn to faint screams.

But if not for me thinking ahead and cheating a bit the Viagra I took prior to,

Now you can definitely have your way and make this dominatrix moment much more true.

When you visibly climax with juices squirting every which way,

Your fourth turn at it is when I finally reach my orgasmic day.

As you collapse on my chest sweaty and warm and imitating an infant,

We truly acknowledge that this is by far the best we've been intimate.

Love or Insecurity

Love or insecurity you be the judge,

As I roll over in bed that spot is vacant no one to nudge.

The smell has drifted away from her absence I was accustomed to cherish,

As the love that once was now on verge of being parish.

From the touch, the taste, the sound of every breath she made,

Laying upon my chest I felt I had the game well played.

Now as time has gone by her essence no more,

I stay think baby come back baby come back, and not sure when I'll get that knock on the door.

Is she really gone I ponder and think all the what ifs,

As I was her knight her king, she my queen my delightful gift.

Seconds turn minutes to hours to days to weeks on end,

I still desire that one true best friend.

Imitators come and go and think they can hold this throne,

For I've yet to have this goddess on speed dial memorized and no need for contact info in my phone.

Not speaking of anyone in particular just all my ups and downs of love not yet truly found,

For when it's real; for real, for real, we both be standing on common ground.

So, as I seek and desire this ultimate beauty of this woman, I have a spot in my heart,

Where art thou my goddess please release the pause button and press start!!!

Intuition or Intrigue; Searching or Discovery

Let's just say you have an inquisitive mind,

Always thinking what a person is bout to say not being caught off blind.

Instincts of purpose following what's to come,

Is it faith, destiny, or something hidden dark up under the sun?

Often, we show signs of things that aren't what they seem,

Wondering if it's a sign or could it just be a dream.

Hints of things to come good in ways of conception or more,

Could be deception instead for this you must explore.

When it involves the heart one can never be too careful at times we misjudge,

For it could be catastrophic to one's love and this makes it heavy as sludge.

When you mistakenly come across something that can be detrimental to your heart,

It often comes off as a weird feeling nearly taking apart.

When you go looking for something purposely you find what you shouldn't have expected,

When you look for bad things often the result is definitely feeling of being neglected.

As saying goes don't go looking for trouble as you find what you seek,

At times we do and it's hard to turn the other cheek.

So, for those who believe you seek you shall find remember often we do this and it's not what we want to discover,

For sometimes hidden truths are to protect those we call our lovers.

With exception of infidelity that should be addressed the moment it happens and it's better to be upfront,

For trying to deceive it puts you a mental place where it is a string of events to follow you definitely don't want.

Indecent Proposal

You can't love if you can't love yourself,
Might as well put your heart on ice store it on a shelf.
Love has blinded me far too long,
As I come to the realization that I had it all along.
My peeps keep me grounded and my lady keeps me sane,
For I have the love that I could relive over and over again.
So, my lady if its big you want or small; I really don't care,
I'd love you the same; here, there, anywhere!
So yes; let's set a date and confess under God,
For we are to be one and defy all the odds.
You're my one true treasure and this I can contest,
You keep me in good spirits for our love I'd never put to the test.
You're my alpha and omega; sunset to sunrise,
Forever my instant go to never a surprise.
Can it be indecent one will truly know unless they discover the truth,
Is it too soon to ask for happily hand in marriage after just a short while commitments to words "I do!"
So, let's just do us never mind the criticism we endure,
For you love me and I love you and this path were both for sure.

Ingredients for Romantic Pastry

Step 1: Preheat sheets of satin or silk on a queen or king size bed,

Fruits, drink, or weed on nightstand for pleasure is more than in your head.

Step 2: Nice hot shower or jacuzzi bubble bath to set your body at ease,

For him, his yack and cigar, for her wine and rose petals aiming to please.

Step 3: Nice hot meal of his/ her meat of choice tasty and tender,

Hot oil rub down the massage is exciting and has its own agenda.

Step 4: A lil dessert of feeding them that fruit that got y'all wild up,

Ready to explode, no need for a measuring cup.

Step 5: A lick here, a lick there oral to a whole new mention,

Ain't even penetrating yet, and you feel like you in another dimension.

Step 6: The entry point is hot and full of indescribable acts,

Had one or two orgasms already, but this shit here, this shit here; is hard to counteract.

All this and sheets in disarray; bodies full of sweat,
You both say fuck it lets repeat all these damn steps.
To be cont....

No Romance Without Finance

Let's just say you've accomplished so many things throughout your young life,

Only thing missing was that husband or wife.

You've tried dating and no one could measure to what you desired,

Even went as far as place a personal ad for girlfriend/boyfriend for hire.

You're out at lunch one day and run into this remarkable person that catches your attention,

Before you knew it it's 3 months later and you're planning something you didn't think was even possible to mention.

Sparks are flying and you're asking yourself is it too good to be true,

For you both are on top of your game and the next step is easy what else is there to do.

Time with one another you spend countless hours and almost separated at the hip,

From just a simple encounter, turned serious, a lifelong commitment you both agree upon into your relationship.

Few years past and everything seems to be aligned with the stars,

Children come into play when you first met did you see things would go this far.

Now here's the kicker that causes things to go on a downward path,

First it was a write up at work, followed by a suspension that joking about your boss now who has the last laugh.

From a week away it was sustainable as you put away a decent nest egg,

But the target you created on your back you didn't believe you dare peg.

As times get harder more days off you didn't request or was scheduled to be,

Your spouse is working twice as hard, your job is seriously in jeopardy.

The stress is unimaginable and begins to take its toll,

As the future is so cloudy now a new story to unfold.

Once such passion was driven into your spouse's eyes,

The thought and stares you get currently with such dismay and despise.

Love making that was epic sheets needed to be changed daily on your bed,

Now that there's these excuses of why boss did this and that womb filled with webs.

Bills get behind and no longer sharing the same sleeping spot,

It feels as if you're in a homeless shelter alone on a cot.

The boss has finally had it with your issues and can't take it anymore,

He dismisses you and the ride home is by far the longest for you know what is not in store.

Your spouse and you argue to the point the kids call the grandparents and staying away is the best course,

But when the dust semi- settles the only action left is the filing of a divorce.

One gesture of being lively and comical in the office changed your future of finances,

But realistically you changed; your whole life and wish you could be do another sort of dances. Was it worth it; in the end, with losing family, career to odd jobs, to making ends meet,

Now just seeing kids every other weekend and living in a studio apt in worse of neighborhoods barely with any upkeep.

Rejection Is Not the End

Let's say you've had your eye on this guy or gal for some time,

Knowing when it was right and not so right to give them thoughts of your mind.

Knew when it was appropriate to make an advance,

When they were involved and even single; did you know or not when it was your chance.

You notice their movements in such a way you could picture how you'd make them act a certain way,

From the start of their morning, to breaks at work, to capping of the end of their day.

You pictured it so vividly but didn't take a step due to being a coworker in risks of gossip,

But your feeling of lust and genuine feelings for them you feel like it's worth the risk.

So, you have a social-able event where you now have your chance,

An office holiday party is in the midst, and you decide here's now your opportunity especially with a dance.

You approach your crush and start with small talk as your normally do as if on the clock,

The vibe is good, and conversation is outstanding they're not even evident you have a secretive plot.

Time goes on a few cocktails consumed and you can imagine how this evening will end,

No more a crush, coworker, or a distant friend.

You daydream of being in each other's arms in intimate sense,

For what comes next you wish you stayed clear for now you want distance.

As you make your move and start your advance in romantic way,

Their attitude changes from pleasant to abrasive the words coming out you didn't think they'll say.

From looking at you as just a friend not actually considering to be their lover,

Said that being with you is like being their sister/brother.

So hurt you are at the dismissal you leave their side without making a scene,

The hurt you feel is so appalling that all you wanna do is scream.

Home alone yet again as was once was a crush is now a total disgust of eyesight when coming in next workday,

Not even returning a good morning or hello nothing for you to really say.

They look at you awkwardly and say I'm sorry, but I didn't see you in that manner,

You're like mumbling under your breath "child please "where's a giant hammer!

You keep it cordial and just smile and nod and go about your day as if it never existed,

Now you focus on solely your job an opportunity you feel they just missed it.

Months go by and you're glowing from ear to ear talk of all the rumors and so,

For you've found that real love and happy as can be and your crush now has envy for, they're rejection saw you grow.

Side Piece

Going to work, to the gym, bar with buddies same old routine,

Pick up the kids on every other day living the American dream.

Schedule is legit no time for interruptions or foul play,

Doing every little thing right the perfect spouse in every which way.

Ten years into it and glowing and seems as happy as can be,

You'd think this was a spokesperson for a marriage magazine on couple's therapy.

From head to toe couldn't see not one undeniable flaw,

Even fresh out the bed this person looks good, yes exclusively in the raw.

So why is it, one typical day on this regularly scheduled frame,

This fine ass woman is at the gym working out well but with some other dude not her main.

She's lit up like a Xmas tree smiling from ear to ear,

He presents her with this big basket and say thanks for another great year.

She smiles and says you know I can't take this home it will cause heavy commotion,

But babe we done been through this before I got your true devotion.

They leave and rendezvous at the normal time slot of his loft,

Bouncing from wall to wall she's never been workout like this by him before normally she leaves not so soft.

She had to put him at a pause as time draws near,

As she doesn't wanna infringe on her routine his feelings she starts to fear.

He went from an intern at her firm, to her understudy, to now a full-grown partner,

All the teachings she gave him professionally and, in the bedroom, now seem to become darker.

Why she asks herself did she let his flirtation go on and lead to such a thing,

Her husband is accomplishing as well; time, money, great dad, gives her everything.

She couldn't put her finger on it as this dude she just can't seem to shake,

Both of them make her quiver ones her husband the other kind of a mistake.

She knows what she likes and likes to have them both but don't wanna destroy her fam,

She's contemplating how to end it with her side piece all the god damns!!

Hopefully, he takes it peacefully as he knows damn well what it is,

Hell, he's even been to house several times hung with the husband and kids.

Now his fiancé ain't no slouch a Victoria Secrets model and on the rise,

She doesn't wanna blow the cover off this secret it would spoil both their lives.

The tainted schedules, meetings, and after work sessions; lies told to cover this deceit,

How will this story end for this woman's side piece?

Streaming Live

Chapter 1

Is it Xfinity app or something online,
Maybe it's the thoughts racing through your mind.
The possibilities of what I could be doing right now,
Miles and states away trying to find a way how.
You want my touches my kisses and licks to run a marathon on your body,
Let me start with the peck to the forehead to start this party.
Nibbling down your neck I begin to suck softly and intensely to the pleasurable taste,
As I'm patrolling your head and shoulder regions orally, I see the excitement moving as you thrust your hips and waist.
Caress your shoulders and licking moving my way down,
The hickeys you feel on your neck from previous actions you don't even budge a frown.
I come to your breast excited I see they are to get my oral attention,
As your nipples hard and firm, the ice I have in my mouth I please without mention.

Sucking and nibbling your areoles your moans get louder and you caress my head,

Moving slowly down your sides to your abdomen lil beads of sweat form on your forehead.

Chapter 2

As I continue in navel area you slowly push me lower, but I don't give in,

Working my mouth toward your thighs the outer region but you want me to go in.

As u tease with the aspect of what the vaginal licks would be,

My mouth licks all around the lower waist and go down to your knees.

Licking your shins now I have another good treat,

Whip cream and caramel; But not yet as I lick every inch of your feet.

An orgasm from toe sucking and this spot I didn't know exist you mentally say,

Damn this man good he really trying to make me feel some type of way.

Now I gently turn you over and a massage of your back begins,

Not noticing the edible massage oil I'm starting to rub in.

From neck on down to back you're receiving the treatment as if you're famous,

I'm rubbing all over back side yup even the anus.

Chapter 3

From both cheeks I rub in oil oh so smooth,

Your body is starting to converge in some type of special groove.

Fighting so hard to sit still I clamp down my hands on your waist,

As I finish with my oil job to your calves now, I can begin my taste.

Licking back of your neck I work down as I did your front,

Trying to explain this to your girls too many bleeped out fonts.

Moving to your back; oh, how sensitive this region is to simplest touch,

Back to ice in my mouth you want me inside you oh so much.

But I keep you in this position for I have yet to please you in way you can't comprehend,

3 orgasms already you exhale in breathing and this man ain't even went in.

Licking and sucking butt cheeks down to inner kneecap,

Here's and orgasm you've never encountered and like wait I need a recap.

Chapter 4

Now the real fun starts to take shape as I grab my instruments of whip cream and caramel,

4 orgasms in and you're already caught up in my spell.

Only few spots I use them on cause you're already floating like a cloud,

We had to get a room at Aura any other place you'd be too damn loud.

So, my ingredients go on your neck, tits, breast, and ass,

Yup in that order are you truly paying attention to my class.

Neck and tits same as before,

But I haven't even explained what the other two have in store.

Got oil, whip cream, caramel all in vaginal area dripping down like so,

As I begin to lick and suck away mixed in with your juices such a nice flow.

Chapter 5

As your juices flow, I start my double dip,
Back forth up and down licking your ass and clit.
A finger or two to aid in my plan,
You feel like you've traveled from here to the River Grand.
So many ways I've made you come and ain't even penetrated with my penis,
A dream you think to yourself he gotta be a genius.
Nope just a man that takes pleasure in making sure the woman I'm with has all her needs met,
This should be illegal or gambled like a Vegas bet.
But back to the exotic erotic moment you're enduring oh so good,
You clamp your hips around my head as if I was wearing a hood.
My lips so soft and sucks got your clit nice and tender,
My fingers inside both wholes and body begins a tremble.
You scream loud the music can't even withstand,
It's like a rock concert at an arena loud as hell with thousands of fans.
The orgasm right now better than the rest,
As you cum you squirt out all types of juice from my head dripping to my chest.
I don't back down I take it all in,
Swallowing every bit, I could muster we both in a win.

This is the end of my oral story and now the break is at hand,

When you come back to strength your thoughts are like damn "wonder what's in his pants?"!!'

The Crush

Seen you from across the room but yet so far away,

You make get big and whispers of naughty thoughts from what everyone had to say.

You come off as stern and take no bullshit is your demeanor,

Wish I can honestly say to myself yes, I have seen her.

You give off such a strong presence that can come off as being stuck up,

But it's from the outside looking in and don't really know what's up.

Your beauty is unprecedented and the body that could knock down doors,

You command attention in any room make all men drop to the floors.

Is it the peanut butter/ butter pecan complexion that accents your gorgeous features?

Or the shoe game I notice on you that you're a formidable creature.

All of the above; your heavens above the rest,

Your beauty is by far immaculate indeed deserve your own crest.

Who are you they wonder the crush that has me in such a daze,

But wait there's competition that I can't quite complete this phase.

She is exquisite indeed and yet her darkness is silky smooth,
Body like the other but she has her own type of groove.
Both are the best and share only one comparison,
They are my crush each a different topic of discussion.
So, I'm come forth and let the record be set straight and clean,
My crush is none other than the daughters, sisters, nieces, aunts, moms, and grandmothers of that the Ebony/ African American Queen!!!

Wandering Eyes

Just like the saying goes just because it looks good, it ain't always good,

But there is this new hot young thing that just moved in the neighborhood.

5'3" about buck 30 and curves out this world,

Eyes legitimately green natural hair in curls.

Divorced so you heard bearing one child,

Just the look of her when she pulls up drives all the neighbors wild.

Astonishing beauty all the wives take notice and remind their husbands not to get too friendly,

For the self- perseveration takes over and soon she becomes new public enemy.

Most of the people reside here are all happily married couples 30s-40s with a splash of a few seniors,

She has brought a dilemma to the block club just for being single with that single demeanor.

Nothing she has done directly to offend just being courteous and speaking and little small talk here and there,

But jealousy within younger wives take notice and soon begins the fear.

But as she needed help of the handyman electrical kind,

Sadly, to say there's one amongst this group and soon everyone's attitudes began a change of mind.

He reluctantly takes the job after his wife and others debate,

For what happens next is soon to be more than faith.

As he does what he's hired to do without any complications,

She starts a conversation that bothers him dearly and soon it becomes apparent her move is a unique situation.

She was married to a real estate broker, so she thought, and their life was considered a dream,

From a small town she came from he was a city guy, but hidden secrets began the screams.

Met in college and soon engaged and exchange of vows shortly after degrees received,

She thought the lifestyle they were living was from his long hours and hers; but she was greatly deceived.

He had a hidden agenda and another personality that didn't match how they lived,

For it was discovered when she gave birth to their daughter such a gorgeous kid.

The baby shower had produced such an array of different characters from whence she had unknown,

Now his trips to the Middle East had really become apparent and her mind totally blown.

For he was from an exiled royalty that became nonexistent to torture and murders alike,

Fearing what could happen to their family his father became close with UN and the USA was there first flight.

Spoke perfect English so to this she was totally ignorant,

But because of the child's blood line being mixed a divorce was the only settlement.

Fears for the lives of his wife and infant daughter after his father's untimely demise,

He couldn't allow anything after the assassination of his dad to cause any further cries.

He had to return to his homeland to become king of this rich province to fully accept the crown,

But due to his loyalty to his country and people being married to a foreigner against their culture he prevented any frowns.

He told her give him time as he wanted to fix the issues that occurred through this tragedy,

He was truly all about being loyal to his country and even more to his family.

She couldn't stand by and wait for time that was not determined,

Instead, she went into hiding changing her name for safety and now just still being a surgeon.

So as the electrician went back to his wife with the news that bothered him so,

Wandering eyes became a counsel of worried sisters and brothers that now looked out for her and help her grow.

I CAME; DID YOU

Good morning, I say to her as she walks past me every day,
Her persona and style are different something like an Expose.
She's the epitome of classy soulful and full of grace,
Dressed up or dressed down sexy with just the right hint of taste.
So, I take the courage to say more than just a greeting and spark this one in a million conversation,
For what happens next, I didn't see coming or prepare for this situation.
As we begin our talk, who would've thought it, we've known each other for years,
As we graduated the same class back then she was considered the nerdiest of our peers.
Me I was known but more so as a clown type,
As we begin getting in depth, I was waiting for the sound bite.
We both had to rush to our prospective employers but maintained communication along the day,
Telephone, fax, text, emails, we did it all throughout the course of our day.
She said she maintained her single life once she realized who I was on the train,
Hoping that one day I'd break the ice to have her feeling that way again.

I'm dumbfounded for sec and looking at her like whoa!
What is it you speak?

She said from way back when I had the voice and every word out my mouth was the only way to get her knees weak.

So, I'm in awe, shocked, stuttering with my words now, and starting to work a sweat,

Are you saying that since we were teenagers that you've had this thing for me that you could never forget?

So, she agrees to every last content that my voice had a way with her that trembles her soul,

That gets her an outer body experience she's never had something like fool's gold.

So again, I'm lost and questioning her context to what she truly means,

She explains to me that every man she's dated has never did what I did, and truly made her cream.

I'm like wait a minute before we get off this train, I'm single now so how about you,

Let's stop talking about this shit, and "make it do what it do!"

She explains to me not tonight some other time I have to go take a long hot bath,

I'm like what the hell was all that for; she just stands there and start to laugh.

I don't see shit funny; are you playing some twisted sick joke and shake my head,

As I walk her to her car, she places my hand under her skirt gently between her legs.